Textin Text

Contents

ROC

by Anthony Masters

> **URGENT**
> **C U @ THE BEACH**
> **SEAN**

Ben glanced down at his bleeping mobile phone. It was seven o'clock on a Saturday morning and he was desperate for more sleep. But the text message said *urgent*, so Ben dragged himself out of bed and got dressed.

Outside he mounted his bike and rode down to the beach. Sean was sitting in the sand dunes, looking excited.

"I was about to send you another message," shouted Sean. "Some weird lights appeared last night. I suspect something landed on the beach."

Ben was reluctant to believe him. Sean was always playing the fool and making up crazy stories.

"Now I've discovered something," Sean continued. "Come and take a look."

"What is it this time?"asked Ben.

"There. What do you reckon?"

"Not a lot," said Ben. "You've hauled me out of bed to gaze at a hole in the sand."

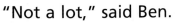

"Feel the heat!" said Sean excitedly.

Ben touched the sand. It did feel warm.

"Let's start digging!" said Sean. "I'll zip back to the house and fetch some spades."

"Don't bother," said Ben. "It's just the heat from the sun." He remounted his bike. "I can manage without a morning's digging. We're in a football match this afternoon, in case you'd forgotten?"

But Sean was already running back to his house nearby. "I'm getting a spade. See you at the match."

As Ben arrived home, another text message made his mobile bleep. This time it was from Sean's younger sister.

> SEANS GONE WEIRD
> CAN U COME OVER
> KELLY

"Going out again?" asked Mum, as Ben wearily wheeled out his bike. "Where to this time?"

"I'm going to Sean's. Kelly says he's acting weird."

"So what's new?" Mum said.

Ben arrived to find Sean wandering from room to room. He was spouting nonsense in a strange high-pitched voice. Several times he bumped into the furniture and almost tumbled over.

Kelly was pretty upset. "He's been like this ever since he came back from digging on the beach," she said. "It's a good thing Mum and Dad are out shopping."

"You know what he's like," said Ben. "He's just mucking about."

He walked over to Sean and shook him. "Stop this now!" he yelled. "We've got an important match this afternoon. Snap out of it!"

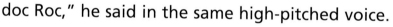

But Sean just looked puzzled. "Zot wofor pran doc Roc," he said in the same high-pitched voice.

"Knock it off!" Ben demanded, shaking him harder.

But Sean just continued talking rubbish and wandering around the house.

Ben and Kelly went outdoors.

"Are you sure he's OK?" asked Kelly.

A cloud of sand blew off the beach in the strong wind. For a moment, Ben thought he could see something metallic in the sand, glinting in the sunlight. When he looked again, all he could see was sand.

"Of course he's OK," Ben tried to reassure her.

"He doesn't usually play a joke for this long. He's just trying extra hard to wind us up."

It was nearly half-time and the score was 3:0.

"This is crazy!" yelled Ben. "What on Earth are you doing, Sean?"

Normally Sean was a brilliant striker, but this afternoon he hadn't scored a single goal. In fact, he was behaving as if he'd never kicked a football before.

"I am the ball follow," he muttered in his high-pitched voice.

"What?" shouted Ben.

As the half-time whistle blew, the team gathered round.

"You're rubbish!" said Paul Jenkins, scornfully.

"You're throwing the match away!" shouted Bob Simpson, their coach. He was furious.

"He's rubbish!" repeated Paul.

"Not," said Sean.

"Get stuck in then!" said Bob.

The whistle blew again, but Sean played just as badly as he had in the first half. By the end of the match, they were six goals down.

Afterwards Sean strode off the pitch, jumped on his bike, and rode off as if he couldn't care less. As the rest of the team left the field, Ben reckoned the joke had gone too far. Much too far.

That evening, Ben picked up another text message.

COME 2 THE BEACH
IM TRAPPED
SEAN

"Sure," said Ben to himself. "You won't get me going this time, Sean." And he sent Sean a rapid response.

U WRECKED THE MATCH
QUIT BEING AN IDIOT
BEN

Sean messaged him back.

IM NOT JOKING
COME 2 THE BEACH

Ben's face was red with anger as he strode through the kitchen. "Sean needs sorting out!" he growled.

"About time someone did," sighed Mum.

Just before he got on his bike, Ben sent a text message to Kelly.

Ben rode towards the beach. When he arrived, he saw that Kelly had messaged him back.

> SEANS AT HOME
> DO U THINK HES LOSING IT
> KELLY

Ben turned and headed for Sean's house. What was going on? How could Sean be both at home and at the beach?

Kelly immediately answered the door. She looked puzzled.

"*I've* also had a message from Sean saying he's at the beach and to come urgently," she said.

"You said he was at home."

"He is!"

"How can he be...?" Ben paused and hurried past her into the hall.

Sean was standing on his head. "To you to this?" he asked.

Kelly grabbed Ben's arm. "I don't like this," she said. "Let's go down to the beach."

"What for?"

"To see what's going on."

13

"I wonder why Sean said to come here urgently?" Kelly pondered, as they reached the beach.

"He said he was trapped. He's certainly taking us for a ride this time!" said Ben.

They dismounted their bikes and checked out the dunes. Nothing unusual to be seen.

"Hold on," said Kelly. "I'll call Sean on his mobile and ask him what all this is about. Why didn't I think of that before?"

Sean answered the phone at once. He sounded dead scared.

"It's *Kelly*, Sean. Are you at home?"

"Of course I'm not at home!"

"Then wherever *are* you?" Kelly was beginning to lose her temper.

Ben took over. "What *are* you playing at, Sean?"

"I'm not playing – I've been trying frantically to phone you, but the battery's low." He sounded desperate. "You've got to believe me. I'm in a pod."

"In a what?"

"I found this pod buried in the dunes – where I saw the lights come down."

"Pod? What's a pod?" asked Ben. He no longer thought Sean was joking. In fact, he was afraid.

"It's a small spacecraft from an alien mother ship. The mother ship is hovering just above Earth," Sean explained.

"*What?*"

"There were twelve pods for twelve students from a school on Jupiter. I met one of them. He's called Roc. They frequently make trips to Earth to check out the planet, and then they return to the mother ship. They were all instructed not to land, but Roc crash-landed his pod when the hyper-drive failed."

"Where are you?" asked Ben urgently. "Just give us your *location*."

"I told you. I'm in the pod."

Then the line went dead.

"So where is he?" asked Kelly, now more than a little scared.

"In a pod."

"But how can Sean be at home as well as in a pod?"

"I don't understand what's going on, but Sean's in some kind of trouble," Ben responded. "We need to find him – quickly."

Their continued search of the dunes still turned up nothing. Was Sean really winding them up after all?

"OK," Ben said. "I think we've been had. Just wait till I get my hands on that brother of yours."

Just then, Sean himself walked out from behind a sand dune.

"Is this what you're looking for?" he asked.

"Sean? What's going on?" asked Kelly angrily. "Why did you tell us you were in a pod?"

Sean ignored her. He got down on his hands and knees and began to clear away the sand to reveal … the rim of a large silver disc.

Ben gasped.

So did Kelly.

"What on Earth –" started Ben.

They crouched down as Sean continued to clear the sand away from the disc. It was about the size of a small car.

"Wow!" said Ben. "I can see Sean."

"Of course you can!" hissed Kelly. "He's standing right beside you."

"Is he? Come over here and take a look in the cockpit."

Kelly looked. "I don't believe what I'm seeing," she cried. "There must be ... two Seans!"

Ben and Kelly looked from one Sean to the other. One was trapped in the cockpit of the pod, desperate to get out; the other was standing right beside them.

Kelly's anger evaporated. Now she felt panicky.

"Who *are* you?" she asked the Sean standing beside them.

"I'm Roc," he said. "I'm from Jupiter. My people can change shape. Talking's more difficult, but I think I speak your language better now."

Ben looked at Roc closely. His eyes were large and dark with tiny pupils. The eyes were alien, quite different from Sean's. Apart from that he looked exactly the same.

"I crash-landed," said Roc. "And Sean found me."

"But why take him prisoner?" asked Kelly fearfully.

Roc shrugged. "It was the chance of a lifetime – to be on Earth for a few hours."

"You've got to let him go," demanded Kelly.

"Don't worry. I'm going to," said Roc. "I need to fix the hyper-drive and return to the mother ship."

Roc walked across to the pod, pushed at a panel, and the cockpit slid open. Quickly, Sean squeezed out and Roc took his place behind the controls.

"He kidnapped me!" shouted Sean. "Just so he could take a look at Earth. I thought I might be left in there for ever. And you two were useless! Didn't you guess that Roc was an alien who could change shape into a human being – into me?"

"Er … no," admitted Kelly.

"Perhaps we should have," smiled Ben. "Roc wasn't much of a footballer!"

Roc looked up from the control panel. "I've mended the pod," he said. "Now I've got to go." With that he closed the hatch.

"Look!" shouted Sean. "Roc's face is changing. He doesn't look like me anymore."

They all stood watching as Roc slowly changed shape into a small frog-like figure. It waved as the pod began to lift off.

They all waved back. Even Sean.

Soon the pod was a tiny light in the night sky.

"I'll tell you what," said Sean.

"What?" asked Ben.

"I'll never invent another story in my life."

"I should hope not," said Kelly.

They all gazed up at the sky. There were no lights there now. Only stars. Then their mobile screens – all three of them – lit up with the same text message.

> THANKS 4 HAVING ME
> ON EARTH
> ROC

HELLO, IT'S ME!

by Simon Cheshire

Ryan played practical jokes – constantly. He was only ten years old, but he was the sneakiest kid in the school.

Once, he'd posted a photo on the Internet of the head teacher taking a nap in his office. On another occasion, he'd made the local paper believe that the school was a training camp for spies.

So when Ryan received the first strange text message, he thought that someone was playing a trick on *him* for a change.

His phone beep-beeped its usual tune. He didn't mind that it was beep-beeping in the middle of Maths, but Mr Noseby did.

"Ryan Scroggs!" growled Mr Noseby, peering over his specs. "Is that a phone I can hear, or have you got a musical belly button?"

"Musical belly button, sir," said Ryan, as he pulled the phone from his pocket and hushed it up.

"Well kindly remember that musical belly buttons are against school rules," said Mr Noseby. "As are phones. Now, to return to the lesson ..."

Ryan checked the message.

WARNING
BEWARE SHORT ST
GO HOME A
DIFFERENT WAY
FROM A FRIEND

Pretty poor joke, thought Ryan. Not even funny. So he ignored it.

Short Street was very long. It was slap bang in the middle of Ryan's way home. So down Short Street he went, minding his own business. He didn't notice Gripper, the school bully – until it was too late.

Ryan was halfway down the street when Gripper came out of the paper shop with a copy of *Tough Noisy Motorbikes Monthly* under his arm (which had a copy of *Yippee!* comic hidden inside it). Gripper spotted Ryan in the same instant that Ryan spotted Gripper. Ryan was relieved that he was across the street, so he had a head start. Gripper was relieved that Ryan couldn't see his *Yippee!* comic.

The chase lasted for two roads and a roundabout. Ryan wasn't a good runner, but he managed to stay ahead of Gripper. Someone built like a dustbin, as Gripper was, couldn't take corners as quickly as Ryan.

The school bully gave up after he lost sight of Ryan near the greengrocer's. He stood looking up and down the pavement for a minute or two, then got bored and plodded away.

The greengrocer came out of his shop, spotted a tuft of hair, and hauled Ryan out of the sack of potatoes he'd been hiding in. All the way to his front door, Ryan could hear the greengrocer shouting about young hooligans and how he blamed the parents.

It was after teatime when Ryan remembered the text message. 'Go home a different way' it had said.

Ryan was puzzled. Who could have known that he'd bump into Gripper? Unless Gripper himself had sent the message?

No. Impossible. Gripper couldn't spell any words with more than four letters.

So … ?

Ryan shrugged. It was just one of those unsolved mysteries.

But the following day it happened again. Beep-beep during the lunch hour. Ryan was halfway through a fish finger, and nearly choked when he read the message.

TOLD U SO
2DAYS TIP
BRING PACKED
LUNCH 2MORROW
EAT OUTSIDE OR
GET WET
A FRIEND

Once again, there was nothing to show who'd sent it.

Ryan glanced around, watching to see if any kids gave themselves away by giggling.

Nope.

The following morning, Ryan was faced with a choice. Either ignore the message and risk getting wet, or do as the message suggested. He decided to take sandwiches. He reckoned that if he was going to fall for someone's silly joke, at least he wouldn't go hungry.

At lunchtime, he sat at one of the tables outside the canteen. There was always a

crowd of kids there – mostly those who hadn't finished their homework. They sat emptying their lunchboxes into their mouths with one hand, and writing with the other.

Ryan whispered silly comments to put them off their work.

"Awww, stop it! Look, I've written 'the Tudors were *ding dong boing splat*' now!"

"Ryyyaaaaaan!"

Ryan had almost forgotten why he was there by the time the canteen doors burst open. They burst open quite often – usually to let out floods of kids trying to escape the smell of school meat pies. Today, however, they let out a flood of kids and water.

There was a thick mains pipe that ran through the school canteen. This pipe had been on the caretaker's 'must repair' list since the autumn term of 1993. It had now finally burst, sending a torrent of freezing water across the canteen floor, which soaked everyone in its path.

Must repair

✱ mains pipe
✓✱ lights in room 2
✱ sink in art room
✓✱ hall doors
✓✱ window in staffroom

The message had been right. Again.

Maybe the message was from someone who had made the pipe burst, thought Ryan. But it wasn't possible. The pipe was in clear view of everyone. Someone mucking about with it would have been spotted.

There was only one explanation. Ryan was getting text messages from someone who knew the future.

Hmmm. Spooky.

Ryan took out his phone and looked at it carefully. He switched it on and off a few times. Then he gave it a shake. Then he sniffed it. Everything seemed normal.

Then, beep-beep! Another message came through. Ryan almost dropped the phone with fright.

TOLD U SO
R U GOING 2 PAY
ATTENTION NOW
A FRIEND
PS WORKED OUT
WHO I AM YET

No, he hadn't. Whoever was doing this was obviously as sneaky as he was. But he wasn't about to let anyone get the better of him. Whoever it was had better watch out.

Ryan was feeling so cross about the messages that he deleted the next one. A daft thing to do, because it had all the answers to the following day's surprise Maths test. He hadn't twigged at the time. It had just seemed like a string of numbers.

Once the test papers were given out, and everyone was head-scratching and lip-wobbling, Ryan did some serious thinking.

What was it? How had it gone? 243 ... 19 ... C ... Yes, that fitted the questions. 108.2? Or was it 102.8?

In the end, he remembered 13 answers out of 20.
It was much higher than his usual Maths scores.
Mr Noseby was sure Ryan had cheated.

Ryan, meanwhile, was happier than
a toddler in a bucket of jam. And he
was even happier after break on Friday.
Why? Because not only did he know
that they were getting a surprise Science
test, he also knew every answer.

Ryan got full marks.
Mr Noseby was sure he smelt
a rat, but he couldn't work
out how Ryan had done it.

Things went on like this
for a couple of weeks. Ryan
got used to getting messages
about future events, and
everyone else got used
to Ryan's mysterious new
brainpower.

But everything changed on the day of the school trip. Mr Noseby was put in charge of a tour of the local factory. He wasn't keen on going. He was far too busy trying (in vain) to devise questions that Ryan couldn't answer. But the head teacher was fed up with him moaning around the staffroom, so off he was sent.

CyberTek Ltd sounded interesting, but it didn't make androids or high-powered lasers, or do secret work for the government. Pupils entered the steel and glass building expecting to find flashing lights, armed guards, and dangerous equipment which they'd been warned not to touch. They didn't.

By the time they were halfway through the tour, most of them were wishing they were back at school, having a surprise test on the Tudors. They were going along a high walkway, above lots of dull, grey machines which hummed.

"All these you see," said Mr Noseby, "are filled with magnetic fields and such like, and they program the chips which go into washing machines and mobile phones. Fascinating, isn't it?" But the only person really listening was himself.

Ryan checked his phone for messages. Nothing.

And then it happened.

Maybe his fingers slipped. Maybe Mr Noseby put him to sleep for a second or two.

He dropped the phone.

The phone that had changed his life, the phone that was now the most important thing in the entire world, was falling away from him, down, down, down, clank, bang, smack, into the humming machines.

Ryan yelled.

"Honestly," said Mr Noseby, "the way these children attach themselves to their phones. It's unhealthy."

Ryan yelled again.

The factory foreman fished the phone out just before back-to-school time and handed it to Ryan.

"Fell in the reprogramming system, lad," he said. "Probably got zapped half a hundred times. You're lucky it isn't in pieces."

Ryan tried to say thank you, but only managed a whimper. He went around holding the phone gently in his cupped hands for the rest of the day, as if it was a dead sparrow.

"Pathetic," tutted Mr Noseby.

At home, Ryan finally plucked up the courage to see if it would switch on. "Please, phone. Please don't be broken. Not now. Not after all we've been through. Pleeeeeeease."

The display winked into life. It looked different, more detailed.

Ryan pressed a few buttons. It seemed to be working normally, except that it looked … odd.

The stored numbers were still there, and the ring tones he'd downloaded. And … a whole new menu. Once you scrolled past the usual stuff, up came an option labelled …

TIME > REVERSE

Beep-beep! He almost dropped it again. A new message had arrived.

> WORKED IT OUT YET
> KNOW WHO I AM

"Er, no," muttered Ryan.

> USE YOUR NEW MENU
> SEND A MESSAGE 2
> 10.38 AM
> 22 DAYS AGO
> SEND WARNING ABOUT
> GRIPPER IN SHORT ST
> THEN U WILL GET
> THE POINT
> WILL B IN TOUCH
> A FRIEND

"Twenty-two days ago?"

Ryan flipped through the phone's new options. There was a SEND TO WHAT TIME? and a SEND TO HOW MANY DAYS AGO? He stared at the screen for a moment.

"Okaaaaaay ... Let's see ..."

Then he entered the message.

> WARNING
> BEWARE SHORT ST
> GO HOME A
> DIFFERENT WAY
> FROM A FRIEND

> **SEND TO WHAT TIME?**
> 10.38 AM
> **SEND TO HOW MANY DAYS AGO?**
> 22

"OK. Sent."

So what was supposed to happen now?

Then it finally dawned on him, in one of those flashes you read about, but never expect to come across in real life.

He'd just sent the message to himself. And he'd received it. Himself. Twenty-two days ago. The day of the first message. The day of the message warning him about ...

Beep-beep!

U GOT IT AT LAST
HELLO FROM YOURSELF
IN THE FUTURE
THIS COMES FROM 3 DAYS
IN YOUR FUTURE
DONT 4GET 2 SEND IT

Ryan didn't stop giggling until his parents got worried and threatened to take him to the doctor's.

He had a direct text messaging system that travelled through time. He could tell himself about *anything* before it happened.

Beating surprise tests? No problem! The things he'd be able to do … The jokes he'd be able to play … Things were just about to get interesting …

A MESSAGE FROM XZALTAR

by Brian Caswell

> Lijséfßdç
> lOÓ?ku_hv
> uhlhlAkh{z|}
> Zcv,bl/izdO_
> _kdhf_vpyOv

"What on Earth … ?"

Sarah Connelly stared at the mobile with a frown. What she was reading made even less sense than her brother, Chad. Even when he talked in his sleep in front of the TV, he made more sense than this.

"You've got to stop squinting, Sarah," said her mother, coming out of the kitchen with a washing basket full of rugby kit.

"Mmm. What do you make of this?" Sarah asked, moving across to the washing line, and shoving the mobile under her mother's nose.

"Very nice, dear. Is it new?"

"Not the *phone*, Mother. The *message*. Can you understand it?"

Her mother looked down, squinting the way she had just told her daughter not to. "All this text messaging stuff," she complained. "How you kids can make any sense of it, I don't know."

"That's the point. I *can't* make any sense of it. Chad was in the shower and his phone bleeped, but when I checked the message, all I got was –"

"What are you doing reading Chad's messages?"

"Why not? I'm his kid sister. I'm supposed to do things like that.

Mrs Connelly shook her head.

"Maybe it's a code," Sarah muttered, as she carried the phone back inside the house …

"Touch my stuff again and I'll … I'll …"

Chad always had trouble threatening Sarah. It was easy to threaten other boys. Boys understood threats. But girls … kid sisters … It wasn't fair. They could do things that no boy would dare to. And when you went to threaten them, you realized there was really nothing you could threaten them with.

"And you'll what?" Sarah stood there with her hands on her hips, showing no fear at all. Then she skipped out of the room, tossing the phone onto the bed as she went.

Chad Connelly was rugby mad, twelve years old, and big for his age. That was the reason why he ended up playing in the front row. What Chad really wanted to be was a scrum-half.

"Not that it matters," Sarah said. "When you play for a team that's the very worst in the history of rugby, it really makes no difference where you play. Full-back, right-wing ... or *left right out*!"

The Stranglers ...

Amil Chopra had thought of the name. He didn't play rugby, but he reckoned watching the team run around getting beaten was funny. So funny that everyone on the sideline was choking with laughter.

Choking ... The Stranglers ...

Anyway, Amil had a lousy sense of humour, but somehow the name had stuck. And now they wore it like a badge of shame.

But not for long ...

Chad picked up the phone, twisted the stubby antenna three turns to the right, then two to the left, and pressed the zero.

The screen turned bright red, which made him blink as he read the message.

MEETING ARRANGED
B AT ASSEMBLY POINT
AT 0200 WITH OTHERS
SHIP LEAVES 0205
WILL NOT WAIT

Chad looked down at the phone and thought of Xzaltar, and a smile sneaked over his face.

Not for long …

At one-thirty in the morning, Sarah heard footsteps outside her room. Then Chad stubbed his toe on the cupboard at the top of the stairs. He said some swear words under his breath.

Downstairs, a few seconds later, the front door closed quietly. From her bedroom window, Sarah watched Chad sneaking out of the front gate, then turning left … which could mean only one thing – Sam Greenberg.

Chad and Sam had been friends since the second day of primary school. Sam was in the Stranglers because no other team would let him play – the same reason most of the boys were in the team. Sam's dad coached the team – or tried to. It wasn't easy.

Sarah watched her brother disappear around the corner. Suddenly she realised that she couldn't let an opportunity like this slip by. She quickly got dressed and ran downstairs. Then, closing the front door quietly, she slipped out into the cold air ...

Inside the old glass factory, the shadows clung around the walls, as if they themselves were scared.

Sarah watched through the window as the boys began to arrive. Chad and Sam, and the Jackson brothers, Dan and Pete, stood by the wall. Perry Richards was throwing a tennis ball up in the air and trying to catch it. Titch and Sunil were laughing about something.

The others arrived in ones and twos from all directions, until finally the whole team was assembled. Fifteen boys without any athletic talent between them. Fifteen boys who were tired of being called losers.

Sarah wondered what they were planning. The old factory was huge and empty, and the space where they were standing was big enough for playing a game of rugby ... or landing a good-sized spaceship ... which is exactly what Xzaltar did.

Standing on the windowsill, looking in, Sarah watched the boys spreading out around the walls. I wonder what they're going to do now, she thought.

Then, suddenly, the air began to ripple ... then glow red ... then, a huge silver ... egg appeared out of nowhere.

In less than a second, it was sitting there in the middle of the factory, hissing and gurgling like a pot of boiling porridge. The boys just stood there watching it, like it was the most natural thing in the world to watch a spaceship appear out of thin air.

Then the hatch slid open, and Xzaltar stepped out. He was pretty impressive. Six feet tall and dressed in a shimmering silver … cloud. He gave Chad a wave. Chad waved back.

"Óffleing œ›ëlhgl. Blick!" said Xzaltar.
And Chad replied, "Óffleing œ›ëlhgl. Schleck!"
And Sarah fell in through the window, banging her head on the floor …

"It's not as crazy as you think," Chad explained, as Sarah got to her feet, a bit dazed. "This is Xzaltar," he went on. "We saved him when his spaceship crashed on the field, when we were training. We were the only people around.

"We hid him in Pete and Dan's garden shed," Sam added, "until he could phone home, and get a lift back to Hraltixtz."

"He was ever so grateful." said Pete.

"And he promised to come back and reward us," smiled Dan.

"sssNot ssrewardsss," Xzaltar cut in, sounding like a cross between a leaking kettle and a snake, "sssjustsss a sssthank yousss." Then he shook his head and fiddled with a knob on the side of it. "Stupid translator. It got bashed in the crash, and I haven't fixed it yet."

"The scientists on Hraltixtz are the cleverest in this part of the universe," Chad told Sarah. "Xzaltar told them about our problem. They say they have a solution."

"What problem?" Sarah asked, still confused. Then she noticed that Sam was looking at her and frowning.

"What are we going to do with her?" asked Sam. "It was supposed to be a secret." He looked towards Xzaltar. "Don't you have something you can zap her with, to make her forget the whole thing?"

"I think we should take her with us," Xzaltar replied. "Perhaps she will learn enough to keep your secret."

Sarah looked up at the spaceship. "Just try to keep me off!" she said, stepping inside.

The others followed.

The thing about inter-dimensional travel is that it doesn't take any time at all. One second Xzaltar was saying, "sssHeresss sswe gosss," and the very same second he was saying, "sssHeresss sswe aresss." Then the hatch was sliding open, and they were stepping out onto the soil of Hraltixtz ... which looked exactly like the soil on Earth – except that it was purple, and the worms crawled along the surface. Two suns shone down from a beautiful violet sky.

It was a little scary.

But the boys weren't scared. They were excited.

"Why are they so excited?" Sarah asked, watching, as Hraltixtzian scientists, dressed in white clouds, led them away.

Xzaltar fiddled with the knob on his head again. The scientists of Hraltixtz invented the auto-trainer, especially for creatures with weak muscles. In twenty-four Earth hours, it can turn a ... how do you say it? A wimp into ... well, someone who can hold their head up with pride – in any company.

"Does it work with girls too?" Sarah asked.

Xzaltar smiled. Of course. Follow me...

The disappointing thing about the auto-trainer was that you didn't remember the training.

"Which is just as well," Xzaltar explained twenty-four Earth hours later, as they were lining up, ready to go home. "The machine stretches every single muscle. If you weren't asleep during training, the pain would make your eyes pop out."

After that, no one asked any more questions about the technology.

"Why can't we stay for a while to look around?" Sarah asked.

"Inter-dimensional timing," Xzaltar replied. "If we leave now, we will get back at exactly the moment we left. If we delay, we will arrive home three hundred years in the future."

"Here we go," Xzaltar announced. "Here we are."

And the trip was over.

After a few goodbyes Xzaltar returned to the ship.

"Farewell, young people. And remember, be kind to them," he said. And the hatch slid shut.

Lijs éfßdç
lOÓ?ku_hv
uhlhlA kh{z|}
Zcv,bl/izd0_

A week later, Sarah picked up Chad's mobile, twisted the antenna three turns to the right, then two to the left, and pressed the zero.

The screen turned bright red, which made her blink as she read the message.

GREETNGS EARTH FRIENDS
GOOD FORTUNE IN
THE GAME 2DAY
REMEMBER
B KIND
XZALTAR

"Be kind ..." she whispered. Then she smiled.

"I've been working on a new game plan," Mr Greenberg explained.

It was five minutes to kick-off, and Mr Greenberg began scribbling lines and circles on his tiny blackboard to explain the moves. He thought it made him look like a real coach.

When he had finished, Sam put his arm round him. "You're a great coach, Dad," he said. "And I just want you to know that all the training is about to pay off."

Mr Greenberg felt proud as he watched his players run onto the field. But he didn't hold out much hope. Most weeks, the game was over by half-time.

By half-time, the game *was* over. The Branleigh Tigers, who had only lost one match in three years, were sitting on the field in shock, staring at the scoreboard – 65:5.

After a few minutes, their coach approached Mr Greenberg, and asked if they could call the whole thing off. Mr Greenberg smiled and agreed. The Branleigh coach walked back to his team.

As he crossed the field, he looked at the young girl who was standing where she had stood after the last kick of the match – ten yards behind the goal line. She had caught the ball from a kick, just as the referee had blown his whistle for half-time.

Then, while everyone else was watching the Stranglers celebrating, he saw her kick the ball – a perfect drop kick that scored a drop goal at the other end of the field.

"So what happened?" asked Mr Greenberg, still shocked.

"It must have been the new tactics," Chad said. "I always said you were a great coach, Mr G."

On the side-line, the parents were singing 'We Are the Champions'. Sarah pulled her brother aside. "How come you let them score that try?" she whispered. "You could have stopped that player easily."

But Chad just smiled. "Xzaltar's message," he replied. "He said to be kind."

As Chad went to join in with the team, Sarah stood for a moment, staring at the goal posts at the other end of the field.

What was it Xzaltar had said?

"You can hold your head up with pride – in any company."

Maybe she should take up golf ... or she could become the first female Formula One motor racing champion ... or maybe she could take up rugby ...

Sarah looked across at her mother. Mrs Connelly was frowning, a puzzled look on her face.

"You've got to stop squinting like that, Mum," Sarah whispered to herself and smiled.